KNOW
YOUR
HORSE

Living Horses

KNOW YOUR HORSE

A Medical
& First Aid
Record Book

Monika Rodger

Living Horses

© 2012 by Monika Rodger
© Cover design, Photography & Illustrations: M Rodger 2009

First published in Australia 2009
Revised Second Edition 2012

ISBN   978-0-9806834-5-5

Rodger, M.
Know your Horse: A Medical & First Aid Record Book

Disclaimer Note: The content of this book is intended for information purposes only and is provided in good faith on that basis. The information is intended as a guide only and should not be used as a substitute for advice from your vet regarding the health of your animal. You should never delay seeking veterinary advice based on any information included in this book nor disregard professional veterinary advice based on its content.

www.livinghorses.com

I do not believe that there are any *'hard and fast'* rules when it comes to horses, or that things can only be done in a certain way.

I do, however, believe in having an open mind and being willing to listen to others.

Whether I agree with them, or not, is another matter.

The important thing is that I am always willing to learn more and hopefully make the right, informed, decisions for my horse.

CONTENTS

DEDICATIONS

To my dear friend Margrit.
The time we spend with our horses is always so
special. Highs or lows, they always teach us
something new about our beloved horses,
and on occasion, even ourselves.
We are always willing to learn and be open
to new thoughts and ideas.

And, to my friend Carole.
A true horse woman with one of the biggest
hearts I know, not just for the 'ponies',
but also for her friends.

Most importantly,
To my loving husband Brendan,
for always supporting me in whatever I decide to
do, and often giving me that little push to go
ahead and *just do it*.
Thank you

♥

For me, like for so many others, ever since I was a little girl, it had always been a dream to own my own horse.

Growing up in the suburbs of Frankfurt, Germany, and raised by immigrant parents, I believed that it was an impossible dream for me to achieve. But I still continued to read and learn from any horse related books I could get my hands on, just in case, one day, my dream did come true.

It wasn't until my twenties, living in Australia, and watching the Sydney 2000 Olympics, that my childhood obsession re-emerged and I decided I was ready to own my own horse and start taking riding lessons.

I started having lessons and eventually bought my beautiful mare Abbey, which I kept on a couple of acres next door to my riding school and instructor. I had it great. Easy access to a riding arena, instructor on hand, numerous vets close by, and help when and if I needed it.

A few years later, my husband and I moved to country NSW, and I moved my mare into what seemed to me, at the time, an unusually large paddock of 20 or more acres. In addition, my mare was now also in with several other horses and had to establish her pecking order within a new herd.

My safety net that I had taken for granted was gone. I was now the only person responsible for the wellbeing of my horse with no back up, and I suddenly realized that all the things I had learned, and thought I knew, didn't really help me much when it came to first aid and treatment of my beloved horse.

Sure, I could call a veterinarian anytime something went wrong, and have them come out. But the bills soon add up, and when you do not have a regular income, you just cannot afford that luxury.

With that in mind, I decided I had to learn a lot more about horses than just grooming, tack, riding and what to feed them.

I had to learn more about how to recognize, react and treat injuries and illnesses.

I had to know what was normal, and what could potentially develop into more serious problems. So I enrolled in TAFE (An Australian Tertiary Institution) and began studying a Certificate III in Horse Industry Practices for Performance Horses.

A lot of the topics covered were common sense, but there was so much more to the course that I would never have even thought about. For that I am very grateful and better off. I recommend any potential horse owner to undertake a similar course as it is invaluable.

Which brings me to this book.

As a result of the TAFE course, and being a person who likes to have things organized, I decided to put together this book. I originally began putting this 'notebook' together for myself and my friends, but soon realised that others could benefit from it too.

It can be used to keep a record of your horse's wellbeing, as well as being a handy guide to refer to if your horse does become ill.

Each horse is different, and behaves differently. You cannot be expected to remember everything, especially not in times of an emergency.

I have provided plenty of spaces to write notes and additional information that is relevant to you and your horse. You can also print off, or copy, extra sheets as you need them.

Fill in your horse's medical records & history. Note down your horse's normal behaviour & vital signs. Keep all your emergency phone numbers together.

Most importantly, keep this book in a handy, accessible and safe place.

WHEN SHOULD YOU CALL A VETERINARIAN?

If in doubt...

This can sometimes be a hard question for the horse owner, as we all know that in the case of horses, nothing is small. Especially not a veterinarian's bill.

The good bit of news though, is that you can always call a veterinarian for advice, and that part will usually only cost you the call charge, whilst at the same time it will give you peace of mind.

In time you may build a good relationship with your veterinarian, and find that you can easily call them up for general advice, or to update them on how your horse is recovering.

Your veterinarian will let you know if he or she thinks they should come out, or they will advise you to observe your horse further, and call them back later.

At the end of the day, veterinarians have an extensive amount of knowledge, and are trained to best treat our animals.

...call your Vet!

Calling your veterinarian is one thing, but would you know how to describe the location of an injury accurately?

Learning to identify the parts of your horse is invaluable. It can be especially useful if you are trying to relay information, over the phone, to your veterinarian or other professional.

In the next section you will find some diagrams to help you identify the more common parts of the horse. You can always refer back to them, should you need a quick reference, in the case of an emergency.

There are many in depth and detailed books available, as well as informative websites to visit, which will go into greater detail if you want to learn more.

Remember

If in doubt...call your Vet!

On the following pages are some diagrams labelling the more common points of the horse, hoof, and & lower leg. Try learning them as best you can & refer back to these pages as you need to.

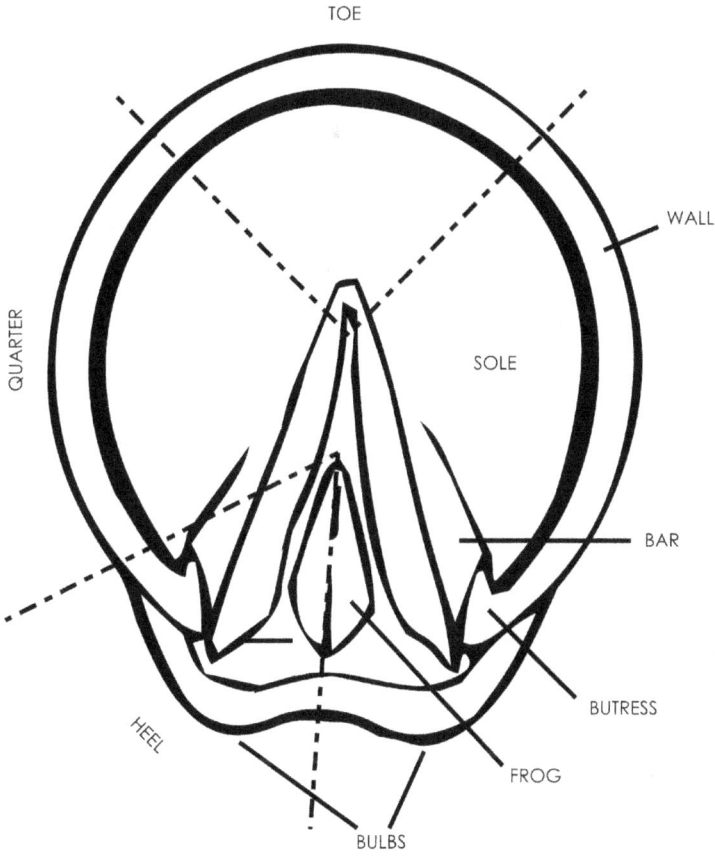

PARTS OF THE HOOF
(Diagram 1)

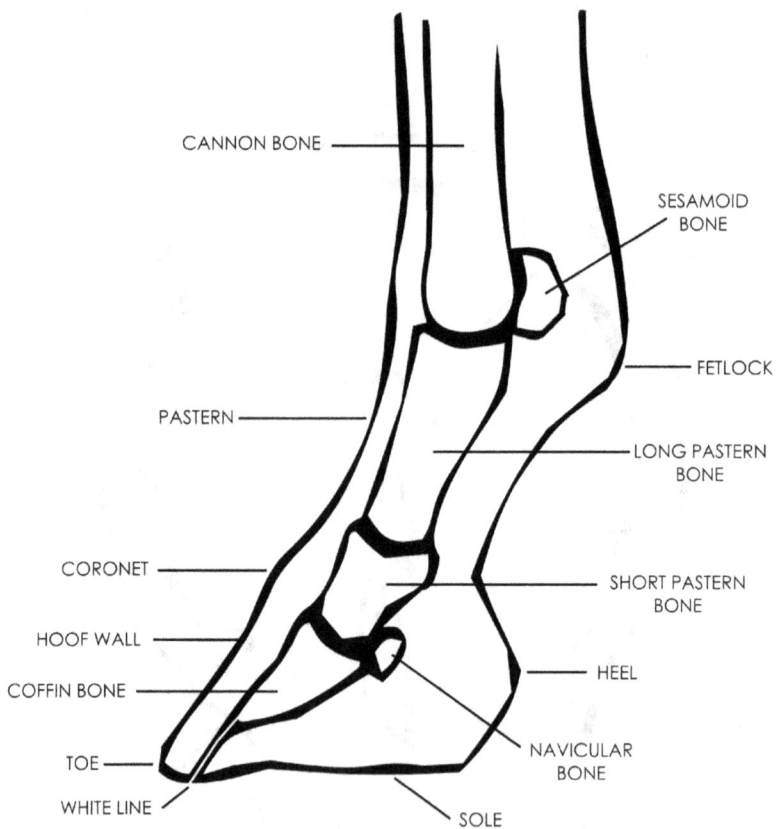

PARTS OF THE LOWER LEG
(Diagram 2)

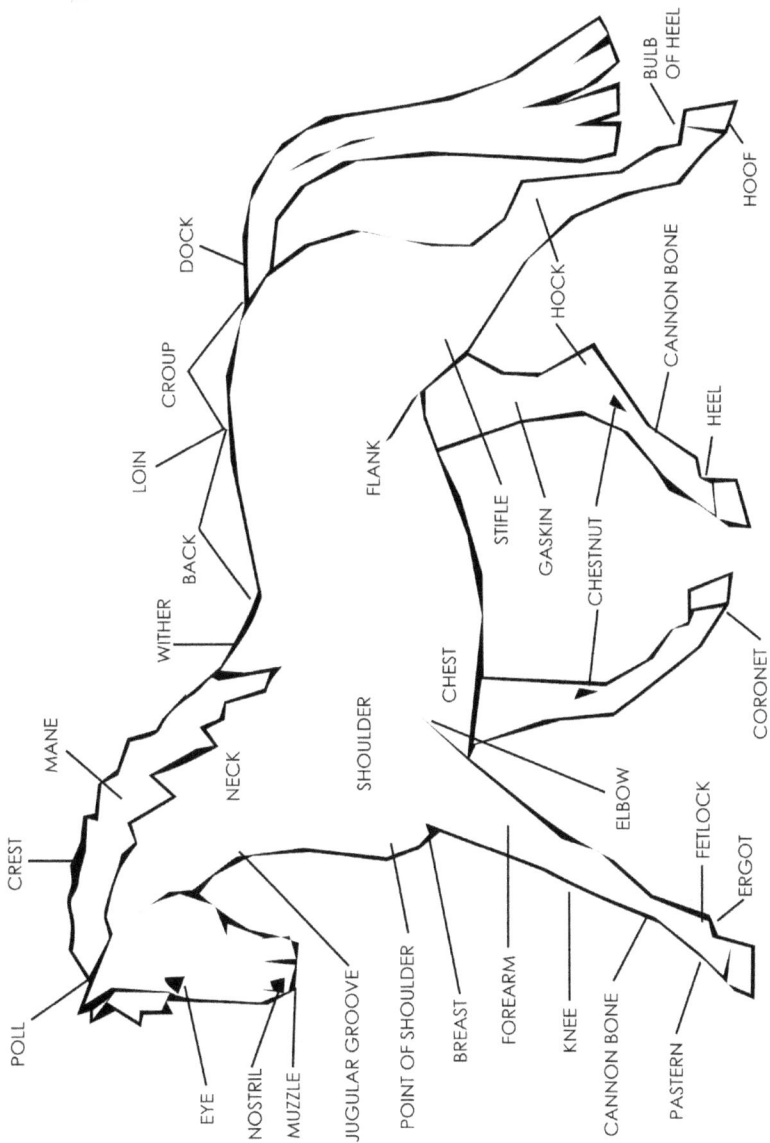

COMMON POINTS OF THE HORSE
(Diagram 3)

Labels in the diagram: BULB OF HEEL, HOOF, DOCK, CANNON BONE, HOCK, HEEL, CROUP, LOIN, FLANK, STIFLE, GASKIN, CHESTNUT, BACK, WITHER, CHEST, CORONET, MANE, NECK, SHOULDER, ELBOW, FETLOCK, ERGOT, CREST, POINT OF SHOULDER, BREAST, FOREARM, KNEE, CANNON BONE, PASTERN, POLL, EYE, NOSTRIL, MUZZLE, JUGULAR GROOVE

FIRST AID ITEMS

In cases of an emergency is it always handy to have a well-stocked First Aid Kit on standby as there is nothing worse than reaching for your kit to find that you don't have what you need.

You can keep your First Aid Kit very simple and add to it as you find you need items, or you could go all out and buy everything you can possibly think of. The latter being a very expensive exercise for items you may never use.

Some of the more basic items to keep handy and to get you started are:

☑ A BASIC LIST OF FIRST AID ITEMS

☐ Head Collar with Lead

Although it may sound obvious, this is one item you don't want to be rushing around trying to find in the case of an emergency. Keeping a set with your first aid kit, or on your horse's gate, at all times is a must.

☐ Pen & Notepad

Essential for writing down vital notes. Keep a few pens & pencils on hand, that way, if one pen doesn't work, you have another ready to go.

☐ Flash light — For night time vision or during power failures

☐ Spare Batteries — For Flash light / Torch

☐ Emergency Contacts — Refer to page 75 in this book for more information

☐ Stopwatch or Watch — With a seconds hand, to time your horse's vital signs.

☐ Gauze, Nappies — Great for applying to open wounds before padding with cotton wool (nappies can work out to be a much cheaper & easier option)

☐ Tape (electrical) — To tape off bandages & keep them from unwrapping.

☐ Large syringes — Useful for flushing out & cleaning wounds, as well as administering oral medication.

☐ Thermometer — To check your horse's temperature.

☐ Stethoscope — To check your horse's heart rate & breathing

☐ Bandages — For wrapping over gauze and wool.

☐ Pliers or To cut horses out of fences, removing
Wire Cutters wire or even loose horse shoe nails.

☐ Mirror A compact make up mirror is ideal
for checking respiration if you don't
have a stethoscope (see page 32
for more information).

☐ Cotton wool With or without gauze. If using
without attached gauze, ensure you
have gauze swabs or nappies to
apply first, so that the wool doesn't
stick to the wound.

☐ Scissors For cutting wool, bandages, tapes...

☐ Clean Bucket

Notes

_____

_____

_____

_____

A MORE COMPREHENSIVE LIST
COULD ALSO INCLUDE THE FOLLOWING ☑

☐ Paper towel — To dry hands, mop up spills.

☐ Alcohol wipes — To clean items / areas to treat.

☐ Tweezers — To remove small items or pick up items.

☐ Surgical Gloves — To prevent spread of infection or seeping of topical drugs.

☐ Bandage Scissors — To cut bandages without poking your horse or the wound.

☐ Surgical Scalpels — For quick, clean cuts to remove skin flaps, etc.

☐ Hoof Pick — To clean out the hoof when looking for causes of lameness.

☐ Hoof Pincers — To help detect pain in the hoof.

☐ Cotton Swabs — To clean out punctures or wounds.

☐ Cohesive Bandages — Used over padding to hold bandaging in place, or as a support bandage.

☐ Bandage Pins — For multitudes of different uses.

☐	Elastoplast Bandages	Used to hold leg bandages firmly in place without the need for pins and tape & prevent slipping.
☐	Hydrogen Peroxide	To rinse out hoof thrush, or to clean / sterilise scissors, scalpels & syringes.
☐	Betadine Solution	An iodine based solution for rinsing out cuts and wounds.
☐	Syringes of varying sizes	To administer drugs, or for flushing out hard to get wounds.
☐	Epsom Salts	For abscess treatment or making up saline rinse mixtures.
☐	Yellow Lotion	Mild anti-bacterial lotion with astringent qualities.
☐	Antiseptic Spray	For topical treatment of infections & bacterial skin conditions.
☐	Honey	Buy it in a squeeze tube for easy application. As above, it can be used on any cuts, wounds, & burns. It can even be used on wounds before bandaging to help with the healing the processes.

☐ Paw Paw Cream   For any cut or wound, similar to honey in its healing qualities.

☐ Zinc & Castor Oil Cream   For topical application to cuts & abrasions, sun burn & dry skin.

☐ Tetanus Anti-toxin   For administering immediately after an injury which results in a break through the skin.

☐ Wet Wipes   For wiping your hands, cleaning around your horse's mouth/ nose/ eyes or under the tail and more.

Hint:

Tick off the boxes as you add the listed items to your First Aid Kit.

And make sure you remember to replace items as you use them.

ADDITIONAL FIRST AID ITEMS

Other Items you may wish to add to your First Aid Kit

☐ _____

☐ _____

☐ _____

☐ _____

☐ _____

☐ _____

☐ _____

☐ _____

☐ _____

☐ _____

☐ _____

☐ _____

☐ _____

☐ _____

☐ _____

☐ _____

☐ _____

☐ _____

☐ _____

☐ _____

☐ _____

☐ _____

☐ _____

☐ _____

VITAL SIGNS

WHAT IS NORMAL?

Knowing what your horse's normal vital signs are, can be very useful in identifying illness, or problems other than the more obvious cuts and abrasions, that tend to jump out at us when we inspect our horses.

It is a good idea to get used to taking your horse's vitals when he or she is healthy and relaxed. Doing this on a regular basis will help you to establish a base line, which you can record on the following pages, and use as reference point if and when needed.

The other advantage of doing this when your horse is healthy & relaxed, is that it will familiarize your horse with the process. It should teach your horse to be more comfortable & trusting of you should you need to take the vital signs when he or she is sick.

It is important to remember that the following ranges are just that, ranges, and will vary from horse to horse and breed to breed.

In time, and with a little practice, you will find that you will be able to check your horse's vital signs with ease and feel comfortable doing so should an emergency arise..

Normal Range of Vital Signs

Temperature   37.0°C to 38.5°C
                         (98.6°F – 101.3°F)
                         If it's over 39.0°C (102.2°F) call
                         your veterinarian for further
                         advice.

Heart Rate   30 – 40 beats per minute

Respiration   10 – 18 breaths per minute

Capillary Refill   2 seconds or less

Mucous Membranes   Should be a healthy, Salmon Pink
                         colour

Hydration   Skin should spring back immediately
                         when pinched.

Note:

Foals & ponies can tend to run a little bit higher
in their vital signs, much like human babies do.

Temperature

Using your thermometer, (you can apply a little Vaseline to the tip for lubrication), stand safely to the side of your horse, and insert it into the rectum, tilting the thermometer a little to the side & up so that it doesn't sit in a stool.

Be careful not to let go of the thermometer, or poke your horse internally.

An elevated temperature may indicate infection or inflammation

A temperature below the normal range may indicate shock, hypothermia or chronic infection.

Hint:
Quite often, if you scratch the base of your horse's tail a little as you go to insert the thermometer, the muscles will relax making the procedure easier.

Respiration

Again, your stopwatch will come in handy, and you can use the stethoscope to make things a little easier still by placing it on the neck and locating your horse's windpipe.

As with the heart rate, you can time their respiration over 15 seconds and then multiply it out by four.

If you don't have a stethoscope you can still take their respiration rate by;

o   Watching the horse's nostrils flare & contract (but make sure they aren't reacting to smells)
o   Watching the flanks as the horse inhales and exhales
o   Feeling their breath by holding your hand up to their nose, or
o   Seeing their breath by holding your mirror to their nose & seeing condensation.

Note:

If using the last two methods, give your horse some time to get used to the smell of your hand or mirror before you start counting.

Heart Rate / Pulse

There are a number of different ways you can measure the heart rate / pulse of your horse. Some more common ways are to:

1. Use your stethoscope to locate a clear spot, just behind the left elbow.
2. Place your finger (not thumb) on the inside of the foreleg where the artery crosses over the bone (level with the back of the knee joint)
3. Place your finger under the top of the lower jaw, pressing the artery with your finger, against the inside of the jaw
4. Place your finger on the artery just above & behind your horse's eye

It is important to use your fingers to feel for a pulse, not your thumb. Your thumb has an artery itself and can cause confusion when you are trying to count your horse's heart rate / pulse.

Count with your stopwatch over a 15 or 30 second period and then multiply up to 60 seconds rather than trying to count for the full minute.

Heart Rate / Pulse (continued)

For example, if you count 8 heart beats over 15 seconds, multiply by 4 to give you 32 heart beats over 60 seconds.

Mucous Membranes

They can help assess how well oxygen is circulating in the body.

The Mucous Membranes include the gums, inner tissue of the eye, and insides of the nostrils. They should be a healthy salmon pink colour and moist.

To check your horse, raise his or her upper lip and inspect the colour of the gums.

Some of the variations and causes can be:

- Very pale pink to white – shock, anaemia, dehydration,
- Bright red – toxicity or mild shock
- Blue / purple - lack of oxygen or delivery of oxygen
- Grey – cardiac problems or severe shock
- Yellow – indication of a liver problem

If it's not pink consult your Veterinarian ASAP.

Capillary Refill

Indicates how quickly the blood returns to the capillaries and how well your horse's circulation is working.

Lift your horse's lip and press your finger or thumb firmly into their gums just above the teeth.

This should temporarily change the colour from pink to white as you stop the blood flow to that area. Now take away the pressure and count how long it takes for the colour to return.

The normal range for capillary refill is 1-2 seconds.

Hydration

The most common way of checking your horse's hydration level is by pinching their skin at the base of the neck, or better still, on the shoulder. (Choose an area that is normally taught or stretched)

The pinched skin should return back to its normal state within 2 to 3 seconds. If the skin stays peaked, or is slow to return, it is a sign that your horse is very dehydrated.

NOTE

By practicing taking your horse's vital signs
when he or she is healthy and relaxed, means
that your horse will become familiar with the
procedures.

Hopefully, your horse will then also be more
comfortable with you taking the vital signs in
times of stress or in an emergency.

HORSE HEALTH RECORDS

The following pages provide you with blank forms for you to fill out as and when you need them.

Use them to record your own horse's resting vital signs, and any other important information you may think is relevant.

This will help to give you a base to refer back to should your horse fall ill, without you having to try & remember what they were at a time when you have other thoughts running through your mind.

Take your horse's resting vitals when he or she is healthy and relaxed, preferably in familiar surroundings. Do this on at least 3 or more occasions, at around the same time each day, to give you a more consistent reading. You can then write these readings on the following page for your records.

I have also included space where you can record your horse's injuries, treatments & outcomes, as well as previous history of illnesses, injury or disease. You can then refer back to this much like a doctor does to a patient's file.

Remember
If in doubt...call your Vet!

NOTES

GENERAL RECORD SHEET #1

Name _____

Age _____ Sex _____

Colour _____ Height _____

Breed _____

RESTING VITALS

Date _____ _____ _____

Time _____ _____ _____

Temperature _____ _____ _____

Heart Rate _____ _____ _____

Respiration _____ _____ _____

PAST HISTORY

_____

_____

_____

GENERAL RECORD SHEET #1

GENERAL RECORD SHEET #2

Name _____

Age _____ Sex _____

Colour _____ Height _____

Breed _____

RESTING VITALS

Date _____ _____ _____

Time _____ _____ _____

Temperature _____ _____ _____

Heart Rate _____ _____ _____

Respiration _____ _____ _____

PAST HISTORY

_____

_____

_____

GENERAL RECORD SHEET #2

GENERAL RECORD SHEET #3

Name _____

Age _____ Sex _____

Colour _____ Height _____

Breed _____

RESTING VITALS

Date _____ _____ _____

Time _____ _____ _____

Temperature _____ _____ _____

Heart Rate _____ _____ _____

Respiration _____ _____ _____

PAST HISTORY

_____

_____

_____

GENERAL RECORD SHEET #3

GENERAL RECORD SHEET #4

Name _____

Age _____ Sex _____

Colour _____ Height _____

Breed _____

RESTING VITALS

Date _____ _____ _____

Time _____ _____ _____

Temperature _____ _____ _____

Heart Rate _____ _____ _____

Respiration _____ _____ _____

PAST HISTORY

_____

_____

_____

GENERAL RECORD SHEET #4

EMERGENCY RECORDS

The following sheets are provided for you to complete in cases of emergencies.

Quite often your vet will ask you for this information over the phone in order to assess how critical the situation is.

By having it all written down you can hopefully relay the information calmly and clearly without holding on to a phone, holding onto your horse, and trying to do your checks as well

Quick Guide

Temperature	**37.0°C to 38.5°C** **98.6°F to 101.3°F**
Heart Rate / Pulse	**30 – 40 beats per minute**
Respiration	**10 – 18 breaths per minute**
Capillary Refill	**1 – 2 seconds**
Mucous Membranes	**Are salmon pink in colour and moist**
Hydration	**Skin should spring back immediately when pinched**

NOTES

EMERGENCY RECORD SHEET #1

HORSE _____

DATE _____

EXHIBITING SIGNS _____

_____

_____

_____

_____

VITALS

TIME	H/RATE	RESP.	TEMP.	TICK IF OK		
				M	H	C

H/RATE	Heart Rate	M	Mucous Membranes
RESP.	Respiration	H	Hydration Status
TEMP.	Temperature	C	Capillary Refill

EMERGENCY RECORD SHEET #1

TREATMENT

_____

_____

_____

_____

FOLLOW UP

_____

_____

_____

_____

NOTES

_____

_____

_____

_____

EMERGENCY RECORD SHEET #2

HORSE _____

DATE _____

EXHIBITING SIGNS _____

_____

_____

_____

_____

VITALS

TIME	H/RATE	RESP.	TEMP.	TICK IF OK		
				M	H	C

H/RATE	Heart Rate	M	Mucous Membranes
RESP.	Respiration	H	Hydration Status
TEMP.	Temperature	C	Capillary Refill

EMERGENCY RECORD SHEET #2

TREATMENT

_____

_____

_____

_____

FOLLOW UP

_____

_____

_____

_____

NOTES

_____

_____

_____

_____

EMERGENCY RECORD SHEET #3

HORSE _____

DATE _____

EXHIBITING SIGNS _____

_____

_____

_____

_____

VITALS

| TIME | H/RATE | RESP. | TEMP. | TICK IF OK | | |
				M	H	C

H/RATE	Heart Rate	M	Mucous Membranes
RESP.	Respiration	H	Hydration Status
TEMP.	Temperature	C	Capillary Refill

EMERGENCY RECORD SHEET #3

TREATMENT

_____

_____

_____

_____

FOLLOW UP

_____

_____

_____

NOTES

_____

_____

_____

_____

EMERGENCY RECORD SHEET #4

HORSE _____

DATE _____

EXHIBITING SIGNS _____

_____

_____

_____

_____

VITALS

| TIME | H/RATE | RESP. | TEMP. | TICK IF OK | | |
				M	H	C

H/RATE	Heart Rate	M	Mucous Membranes
RESP.	Respiration	H	Hydration Status
TEMP.	Temperature	C	Capillary Refill

EMERGENCY RECORD SHEET #4

TREATMENT

_____

_____

_____

_____

FOLLOW UP

_____

_____

_____

_____

NOTES

_____

_____

_____

_____

ASSESSING YOUR HORSE'S HEALTH STATUS

Being able to recognise serious problems and responding to them early can be vital. Although most injuries with horses tend to be obvious cuts, abrasions and lacerations where bleeding is often the tell-tale sign, more subtle injuries, or illnesses, like colic or laminitis can be harder to identify.

For this reason, it is important that as horse owners, we get to know individual horses and learn to recognize their normal behaviour.

Knowing what is normal for your horse can then help us identify abnormal signs including;

- o   A change in demeanour to you or other horses
- o   Moping, lethargy or laying down
- o   Standing away from others
- o   Slowness in reaction
- o   Abnormal stance or not moving
- o   Excessive rolling
- o   Pacing or irritability
- o   Pawing or nudging & looking at flanks
- o   Squinting or tightness in the eyes
- o   Frequent attempts at urinating or defecating
- o   Loss of appetite
- o   Sweating

With time, and as you get to know your horse, you will learn to read his or her normal behaviour, and be able to pick up on changes more quickly.

OTHER UNUSUAL BEHAVIOUR WORTH NOTING

_____

_____

_____

_____

_____

_____

_____

_____

_____

WHEN TO CHECK?

Each and every interaction that you have with your horse can be used by you as a point of assessment. You do not need to catch your horse every time you want to check if he or she is ok. In fact, observing from a distance can sometimes help you assess their health as much as a close up examination.

You can check your horse when:

o Feeding / Rugging
o Grooming – a great time to spot injuries in places that may not be visible from a distance, or if your horse is rugged
o Tacking-up – especially the feet & legs as you clean out their hooves and bandage their legs
o Riding / Exercising – check for stumbling, breathing difficulty, lameness, unwillingness
o Turning horses out, or just passing by paddocks
o Passing by paddocks whether on foot or driving by

Quite often it will be a change in your horse's behaviour that will give you a first indication that something is 'not quite right'. Take the time to investigate it further. If nothing else, it is good practice for you, and your horse, in case something does go wrong.

NOTES

COMMON SIGNS
OF
INJURY AND ILLNESS

A QUICK GUIDE TO HELP IDENTIFY PROBLEMS

Indicators of injury or illness

Abrasions & Lacerations

These are breaks in the skin, bleeding, matting, scabs, swelling. They can occur on any part of the body and be caused by any number of things.

Symptoms are usually wide and varying such as;

- Break in the skins surface
- Some form of flesh exposed
- Possible swelling and heat
- Presence of blood, soreness and / or lameness
- Vitals become affected if infection occurs

Abrasions occur on the surface layer of the skin and normally a thin layer of 'scab' is formed.

Lacerations are deeper cuts where several layers of skin and muscle may be torn and require suturing.

Choke

Occurs when the oesophagus (throat) of the horse becomes blocked by food or a foreign object and the horse is unable to swallow. This can also cause a horse to suffer dehydration if it goes unnoticed.

Symptoms can include;

- Difficulty in swallowing
- Extension of the head and neck
- Feed re-emerging from the mouth and nostrils
- Drooling
- Coughing, deep and throaty, as if trying to clear the back of their throat
- The impression that your horse is going to vomit
- Your horse may panic

Note
Horses are not physically able to vomit.
They are unable to empty their stomachs, in
the same way as humans, which is why colic in
horses can be very serious

Colic

Colic is pain arising in the horse's stomach or intestines.

Symptoms commonly include;

- General unrest
- Repeatedly getting up and down
- Stomping or pawing at ground
- Flehmen response (top lip curling up)
- Excessive or violent rolling
- Looking at flanks or kicking at belly
- Stretching and groaning or yawning
- Attempting to urinate or passing small quantities of faeces
- Little or no sound from the gut
- Depression
- Lack of appetite
- Excessive sweating
- Straining to pass manure
- Not passing manure
- Increased Heart Rate / Pulse

Some horses may exhibit very little to no noticeable signs, but more often than not they will cause a lot of fuss.

Dehydration

Common symptoms can include;

- Dullness
- Sunken eyes
- Lethargy
- Loss of condition
- Thick urine
- Poor performance & recovery
- Tying up

Note

A horse can easily drink 40 Litres of water a day,
and a lot more on hot days or after a workout.
Always ensure that your horse has plenty of
freely available fresh water.

Distress

Common symptoms can include;

- Elevated vital signs
- Sweating
- Lack of condition / performance
- Irritability

Diarrhoea / Scouring

Upset to the digestive tract from various circumstances including, but not limited to, change to diet, stress, infection travel and worms.

Symptoms can include;

- Loose and watery manure
- Foul odour
- Signs of blood in faeces
- Signs of colic, depression or distress
- Dehydration
- Loss of weight / condition
- Elevated vitals
- Decreased or absent gut sounds
- Looking & nudging at flank / belly

Equine Influenza

Is highly contagious and your horse should be isolated immediately to reduce the spread of infection.

Symptoms commonly include;

- A dry cough which can persist for several weeks

Equine Influenza (continued)

- A clear watery nasal discharge turning to thick mucous
- High temperature lasting several days
- Loss of appetite
- Lethargy

Greasy Heel / Mud Fever

Mud fever is usually caused from standing, or exercising, in wet, or muddy, conditions and can be further inflamed by the use of soap and improper drying.

It most commonly occurs in the heel and pastern area affecting chapped, damaged & softened skin created by wet conditions. On occasion it can extend up the legs and to the belly.

Symptoms include;

- Cracked heels down into the flesh
- Inflammation & pink skin
- Raw & bleeding sores
- Thickened skin around sores / cracks
- Infection causing weeping sores

Greasy Heel / Mud Fever (continued)

- Crusty scabs
- Swelling in the pastern & fetlock
- Lameness

Note

Horses with pink skin & white leg markings
appear to be more susceptible to Greasy
Heel / Mud Fever

Lameness

Lameness can be due to soreness or injury anywhere
in the body.

Tell-tale symptoms include;

- Un-even rhythm
- Short stepping or hopping
- Head rising as weight is placed on the sore
  front leg
- Hip dipping as weight is placed on the sore
  hind leg
- Tenseness in the body or an unusual stance

Laminitis / Founder

Inflammation of the sensitive laminae in the hoof and usually present in both front feet.

Symptoms commonly include;

- Severe lameness and a reluctance to move
- Uncomfortable stance
- Short uncomfortable steps
- Reluctant to place weight on the front feet or to move at all
- Heat in hoof with or without an increased digital pulse
- Pain to pressure in the toe area
- Distress
- Increased vital signs

Note

Ponies generally seem more susceptible to founder than horses. An excess of lush spring grass is thought be one cause. Obesity is thought to be another.

Rabies

Is a highly fatal disease that is transmitted by a bite from an infected animal and attacks the central nervous system.

Its symptoms include;

- increased saliva,
- excitability,
- disorientation and running blindly.

Stringhalt

Is a gait abnormality which consists of involuntary and exaggerated flexion of the hocks. It tends to become more evident when the horse is startled, or asked to turn or back-up.

The symptoms in mild cases show a slightly exaggerated hock flexion.

In more severe cases the symptoms show up as extreme hyper flexion of the hocks causing kicking of the underbelly with almost every step.

There is normally no lameness or soreness present.

Strangles

Is highly contagious and your horse should be isolated immediately.

Symptoms can range from very mild to severe and include;

- Swelling of the lymph nodes under the jaw,
- Nasal discharge,
- Fever,
- Increased respiration rate
- Lethargy.

The lymph nodes under the jaw will sometimes swell until they rupture, draining out of the nostrils or through breaks in the skin, and produce a foul smelling odour.

Tetanus / Lockjaw

This is caused by a bacterium that enters the body at the site of a wound like a deep puncture, or in the case of foals, via the umbilical cord stump.

Tetanus can begin with symptoms resembling colic, and be accompanied with stiffness which will rapidly get worse.

Tetanus / Lockjaw (continued)

- Nervousness
- Sensitivity to light, sound and touch
- Stiffness in the front and hind legs
- The third eyelid becomes more visible
- Spasms in the jaw, neck, hind legs
- Sweating
- Laboured breathing
- Flared nostrils
- Erect ears & tail held stiffly
- Jaw locked closed and unable to open

Thrush

Thrush is an infection located in the grooves on either side of the frog. Sometimes the frog is involved.

Symptoms include;

- A foul odour emanating from your horse's foot
- A black sticky substance will be present in the grooves along the frog of the hoof and responsible for the odour
- Lameness may be present in more severe cases

Weight Loss

Can be due to;

- Environment and Climate
- Poor quality or quantity of food
- Bad teeth
- A worm burden
- Chronic pain
- Deficiency in essential nutrients
- Calorie increase to maintain body heat in winter
- Chronic diarrhoea
- Competition for food in a herd
- Bullying by other horses
- Stress
- Digestive tract problems such as stomach ulcers
- Internal abscesses or cancerous growth
- Other illness or disease

Symptoms can include;

- Lethargy
- Depression
- Dullness
- Visible ribs, hips and backbone

NOTES

NOTES

EMERGENCY CONTACTS

Here, on the last few pages of this book, you will find a handy place to write down all your emergency contact phone numbers.

The reason I have done this, is to save you time, when you are trying to locate them in an emergency.

You may also find it handy to keep a list up in your stable for quick access and referencing.

But don't limit yourself to just one, or two, emergency numbers. Write down as many as you can think of, as different people can help you with different problems at different times.

Also keep in mind that you may not always be able to reach your first choice, as they may already be out on an emergency, or out of range.

CONTACTS PHONE LIST

Name   **Phone Number**

_____   _____

_____   _____

_____   _____

_____   _____

_____   _____

_____   _____

_____   _____

_____   _____

_____   _____

_____   _____

_____   _____

EMERGENCY CONTACTS PHONE LIST

Farriers / Blacksmiths   **Phone Number**

_____   _____

_____   _____

_____   _____

_____   _____

Instructors / Trainers

_____   _____

_____   _____

_____   _____

_____   _____

Dentist

_____   _____

_____   _____

EMERGENCY CONTACTS PHONE LIST

Veterinarians   **Phone Number**

_____   _____

_____   _____

_____   _____

_____   _____

_____   _____

_____   _____

_____   _____

_____   _____

_____   _____

_____   _____